I'M ANXIOUS!

LEARNING ABOUT ANXIETY

Katherine Eason

FOX EYE
PUBLISHING

Storms at night made Oliver **FEEL ANXIOUS**. When Oliver felt anxious, his heart beat quickly and his hands felt sweaty. Sometimes, his legs felt wobbly.

Oliver didn't know how to cope with his ANXIETY.

Oliver had a bad dream. He ran down the hallway to Grandad's room. The hallway was dark. Oliver felt **ANXIOUS**. His heart beat quickly. His legs felt wobbly, too.

Grandad read Oliver his favourite book. Oliver **CALMED DOWN**.

One night there was a storm.
The lightning flashed and the thunder boomed. Oliver **FELT ANXIOUS**.
His heart beat quickly. His hands felt sweaty, too.

Grandad hugged Oliver. He said it was okay to **FEEL ANXIOUS**.

Grandad told Oliver that **FEAR** is how our body keeps us safe. He said the storm couldn't hurt Oliver, but his body didn't know that.

Grandad said **ANXIETY** is like a big wave. They could surf the wave until it went away.

Grandad showed Oliver how to **CALM DOWN**. They took big, slow breaths. They pretended to smell a delicious pizza. Then they pretended to blow on the pizza to cool it down.

Oliver **CALMED DOWN.**

The next day, Oliver was going on a sleepover. He thought about that and felt **ANXIOUS** again. What if it was dark? What if there was a storm?

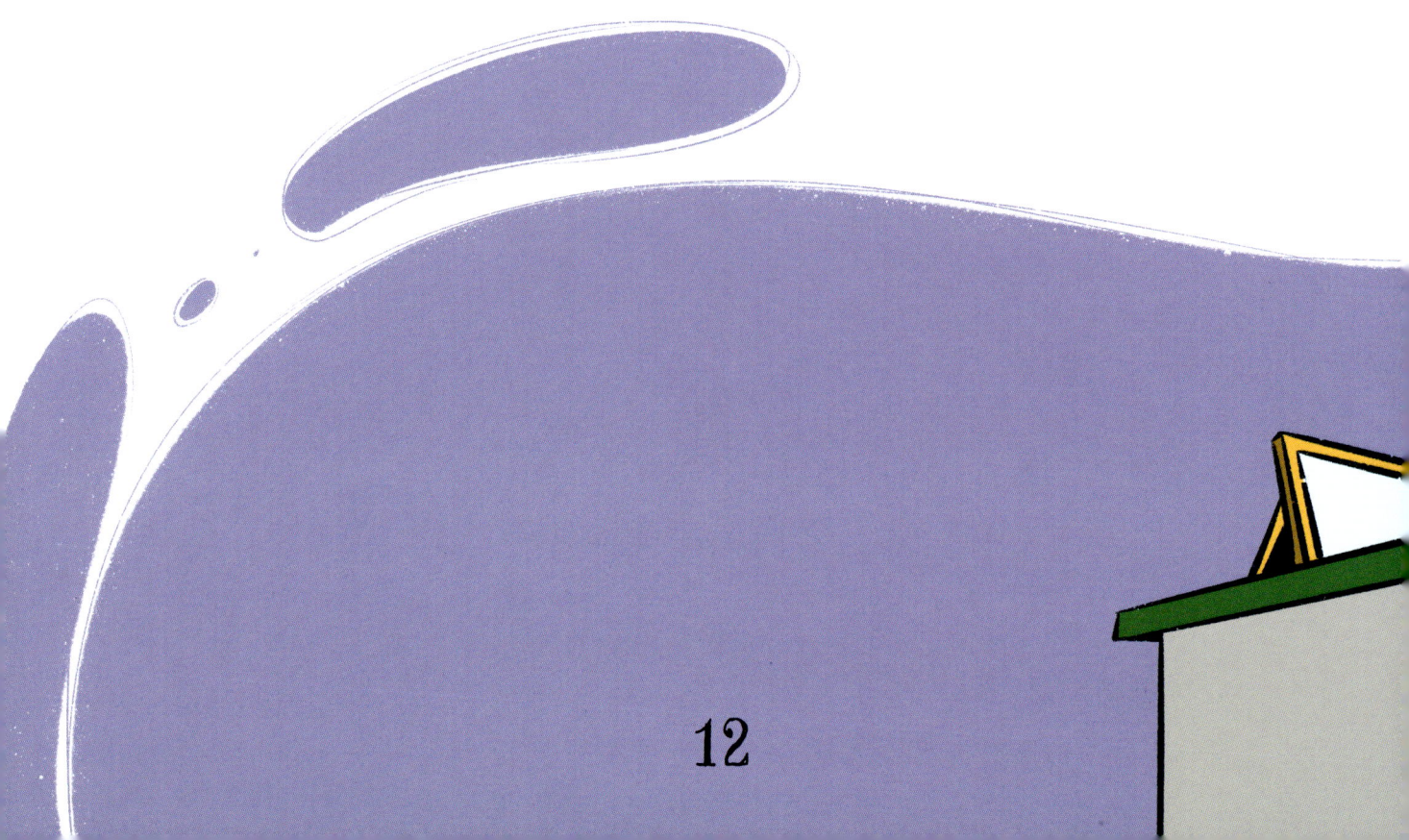

How would Oliver cope with his **ANXIETY** without Grandad?

Grandad hugged Oliver. He said he knew that Oliver was very brave. It might be dark. There might be a storm. Oliver might feel **ANXIOUS**, too. But Grandad knew Oliver could cope with his **ANXIETY** on his own now.

Grandad asked Oliver what he would do if the scary things happened. Oliver thought about it.

Oliver told his sister about what he had learnt. He told her about the book and the pizza. He told her about the wave and the big, slow breaths. He told her about **CALMING DOWN**.

Oliver **FELT GOOD**. He had learnt to cope with his **ANXIETY**.

Words and Behaviour

Oliver didn't know how to manage his anxiety in this story and that caused a lot of problems.

FEEL ANXIOUS

CALMED DOWN

ANXIETY

There are a lot of words to do with anxiety in this book. Can you remember all of them?

FEAR

Let's talk about feelings and manners

This series helps children to understand difficult emotions and behaviours and how to manage them. The characters in the series have been created to show emotions and behaviours that are often seen in young children, and which can be difficult to manage.

I'm Anxious!

The story in this book examines the reasons for managing anxiety. It looks at why calming down is important and how managing anxiety helps people to overcome their fears.

How to use this book

You can read this book with one child or a group of children. The book can be used to begin a discussion around complex behaviour such as managing anxiety.

The book is also a reading aid, with enlarged and repeated words to help children to develop their reading skills.

How to read the story

Before beginning the story, ensure that the children you are reading to are relaxed and focused.

Take time to look at the enlarged words and the illustrations, and discuss what this book might be about before reading the story.

New words can be tricky for young children to approach. Sounding them out first, slowly and repeatedly, can help children to learn the words and become familiar with them.

How to discuss the story

When you have finished reading the story, use these questions and discussion points to examine the theme of the story with children and explore the emotions and behaviour within it:
- What do you think the story was about?
- Have you been in a situation in which you felt anxious? What was that situation?
- Do you think managing your anxiety doesn't matter? Why?
- Do you think managing your anxiety is important? Why?
- What could go wrong if you don't manage your anxiety?

Titles in the series

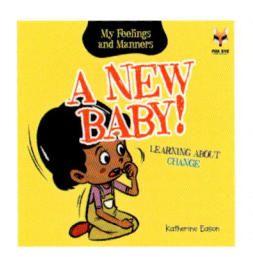

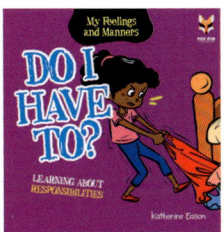

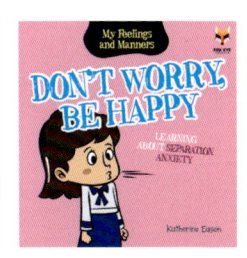

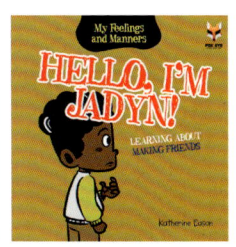

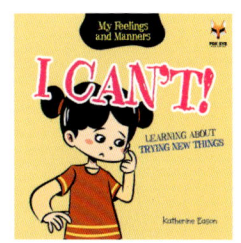

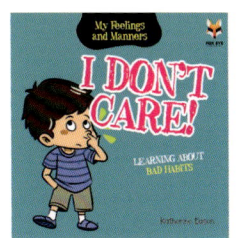

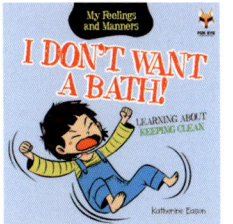

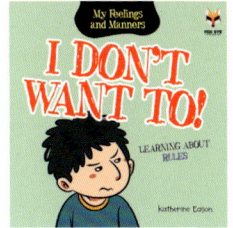

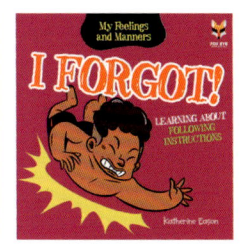

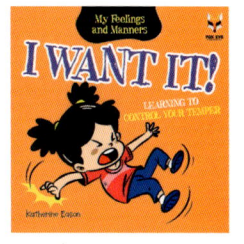

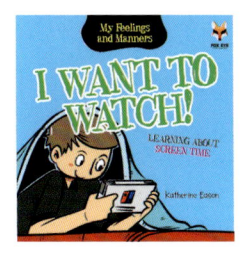

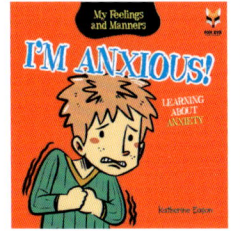

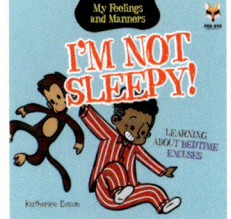

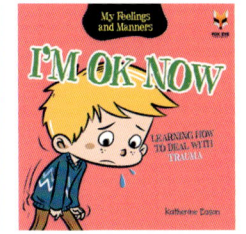

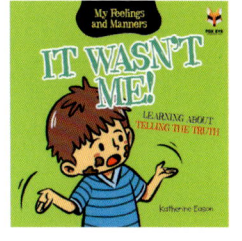

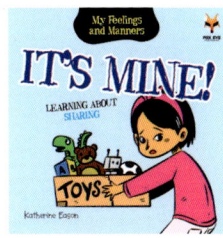

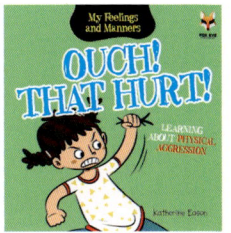

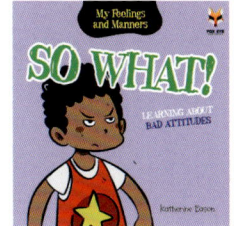

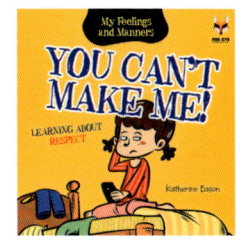

- A NEW BABY! — LEARNING ABOUT CHANGE
- DO I HAVE TO? — LEARNING ABOUT RESPONSIBILITIES
- DON'T WORRY, BE HAPPY — LEARNING ABOUT SEPARATION ANXIETY
- HELLO, I'M JADYN! — LEARNING ABOUT MAKING FRIENDS
- I CAN'T! — LEARNING ABOUT TRYING NEW THINGS
- I DON'T CARE! — LEARNING ABOUT BAD HABITS
- I DON'T WANT A BATH! — LEARNING ABOUT KEEPING CLEAN
- I DON'T WANT TO! — LEARNING ABOUT RULES
- I FORGOT! — LEARNING ABOUT FOLLOWING INSTRUCTIONS
- I WANT IT! — LEARNING TO CONTROL YOUR TEMPER
- I WANT TO WATCH! — LEARNING ABOUT SCREEN TIME
- I'M ANXIOUS! — LEARNING ABOUT ANXIETY
- I'M NOT SLEEPY! — LEARNING ABOUT BEDTIME EXCUSES
- I'M OK NOW — LEARNING HOW TO DEAL WITH TRAUMA
- IT WASN'T ME! — LEARNING ABOUT TELLING THE TRUTH
- IT'S MINE! — LEARNING ABOUT SHARING
- ME FIRST! — LEARNING ABOUT BEING POLITE
- OUCH! THAT HURT! — LEARNING ABOUT PHYSICAL AGGRESSION
- SO WHAT! — LEARNING ABOUT BAD ATTITUDES
- YOU CAN'T MAKE ME! — LEARNING ABOUT RESPECT

First published in 2023 by Fox Eye Publishing
Unit 31, Vulcan House Business Centre,
Vulcan Road, Leicester, LE5 3EF
www.foxeyepublishing.com

Copyright © 2023 Fox Eye Publishing
All rights reserved. No portion of this book may be reproduced in any form without permission from the publisher, except as permitted by U.K. copyright law.

Author: Katherine Eason
Art director: Paul Phillips
Cover designer: Emily Bailey
Editor: Jenny Rush

All illustrations by Novel

ISBN 978-1-80445-167-0

Printed in China